Code It Yourself

ANIMATION

AND PRESENTATION

FROM SCRATCH

An Augmented Reading Experience

By Rachel Ziter

Download the Capstone app!

- Ask an adult to download the Capstone 4D app.

- Scan the cover and stars inside the book for additional content.

When you scan a spread, you'll find
fun extra stuff to go with this book!
You can also find these things
on the web at www.capstone4D.com
using the password: coding.animation

Dabble Lab is published by Capstone Press
1710 Roe Crest Drive
North Mankato, Minnesota 56003
www.mycapstone.com

Library of Congress Cataloging-in-Publication Data
Names: Ziter, Rachel, author.
Title: Animation and presentation from Scratch / by Rachel Ziter.
Description: North Mankato, Minnesota : Capstone Press, [2019] | Series: Dabble lab. Code it yourself 4d. | Series: 4D an augmented
  reading experience | Includes bibliographical references and index. | Audience: Ages 8-10.
Identifiers: LCCN 2018010606 (print) | LCCN 2018012779 (ebook) | ISBN 9781515766629 (eBook PDF) |
  ISBN 9781515766599 (hardcover) | ISBN 9781543536102 (pbk.)
Subjects: LCSH: Virtual reality—Juvenile literature. | Three-dimensional display systems—Juvenile literature. | Presentation graphics
  software—Juvenile literature. | Scratch (Computer program language)—Juvenile literature.
Classification: LCC QA76.9.V5 (ebook) | LCC QA76.9.V5 Z58 2019 (print) | DDC 006.8—dc23
LC record available at https://lccn.loc.gov/2018010606

Designer: Heidi Thompson

Photo Credits
Shutterstock: AlexZaitsev, Cover, Kotkoa, Cover, Phil's Mommy, 6
"Scratch is a trademark of Massachusetts Institute of Technology, which does not sponsor, endorse, or authorize this content.
See scratch.mit.edu for more information."

Printed and bound in the United States of America.
PA017

Table of Contents

What Is Coding?

Playing with an app on your smartphone. Clicking through a website. Without even realizing it, you're using coding. Coding is the language used to communicate with a computer. By creating a set of code, you're writing directions in a language that the computer can follow. Although computers may seem super smart, that's not the case! The only reason computers know how to do anything is because they have been coded to do it. A computer's code—the very specific directions given by a person—allows it to be the super-smart device we all know and love. The reality is, anyone can learn to code. In this book we'll be creating projects using one coding language in particular: Scratch.

What Is Scratch?

Scratch is an online coding platform that uses colorful coding blocks to create everything from games to presentations to animation. The colored blocks are sorted into categories like **Motion**, **Looks**, and **Sound**. By connecting the colorful blocks, you can start coding whatever comes to mind. For example, if you want to code a character to move around and make noise, you would start with an **Events** block, then add a **Motion** block, and finish with a **Sound** block. (You can also use a Control block to make the events repeat as many times as you'd like.)

Scratch runs on Adobe Flash Player, so make sure your software is up-to-date. To download and install Flash, go to: https://get.adobe.com/flashplayer/

TIP:

The projects in this book build in difficulty. If you've never coded before, start with the first project and work your way through. If something doesn't make sense in a later project, try going back to earlier projects to find the answer.

Creating a Scratch Account

To create the projects in this book, you will need a Scratch account. To get started, go to: www.scratch.mit.edu. In the upper right corner, click the *Join Scratch* button.

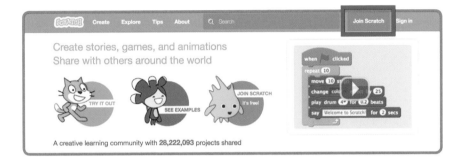

A window will pop up and ask you to create a Scratch username and password. Pick a password you can remember.

It's easy (and free!) to sign up for a Scratch account.

Choose a Scratch Username		Don't use your real name
Choose a Password		
Confirm Password		

The next window will ask for your birth month/year. This is just to make sure you are old enough to use Scratch. If you are younger than 12, you'll need a parent's email to get permission.

Your responses to these questions will be kept private.
Why do we ask for this info ❓

Birth Month and Year	- Month - ▾ - Year - ▾
Gender	○Male ○Female ○
Country	- Country - ▾

The next window will ask for an email address. Scratch will send one email—to confirm your email address—when you sign up. After that, you'll only get emails if you need to reset your password.

Enter your email address and we will send you an email to confirm your account.

Email address

Confirm email address

☐ Receive updates from the Scratch Team

How to Use Scratch

Once you've created your Scratch account, you will see your username in the top right corner of the Scratch homepage. If you don't see your username, you need to sign in. Click *Sign In* and enter the username and password that you've created.

SCRATCH Create Explore Tips About 🔍 Search ✉ 📁 🐱 ⌄

Press *Create* to start working on a new project.

If you've visited Scratch previously, click on this folder to access projects you've already started working on or finished.

You can also search other games and projects on Scratch. This can be a fun way to get inspiration for new projects and see all the possibilities of what can be created in Scratch! Try searching for a project similar to one you'd like to make, then open the existing project to see what code was used.

When you click *Create*, your screen will look like this:

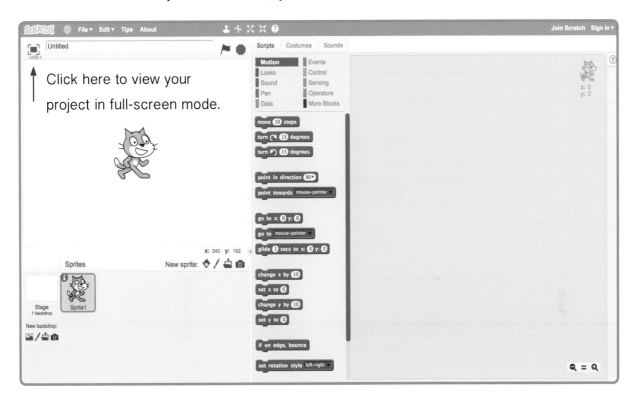

TOOLS

These tools are found at the top of the screen. They are helpful for creating new projects. Click on the tool you want to use—it will turn blue and the mouse will turn into the tool. Then click on the item you'd like to duplicate, cut, grow, or shrink.

 stamp—The stamp is used to duplicate anything in your project. To use this tool, click on the icon so the cursor turns into the stamp, then click whatever you'd like to copy. You can click on a premade character or even a set of code.

 scissors—The scissors are used to delete items in your project.

 outward arrows—The arrows facing outward are used to grow characters. Continue clicking on the character until it is the desired size.

 inward arrows—The arrows facing inward are used to shrink characters. Continue clicking on the character until it is the desired size.

WHAT IS A SPRITE?

A sprite is any movable character or object used in a project. Sprites can be selected through the Scratch Library, created using drawing tools, or uploaded from the computer. Scratch Cat is an example of a sprite!

All sprites can be accessed in this box:

Sprite Library

NAME YOUR PROJECT HERE

This screen shows you what your project will look like when it's finished. In this area you can arrange your sprites on top of your background however you'd like for your project.

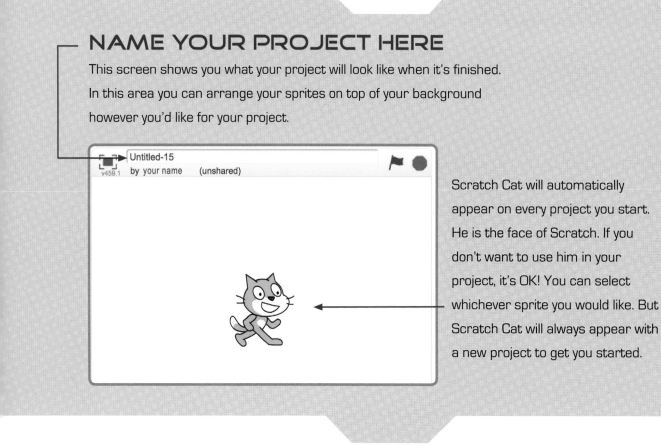

Scratch Cat will automatically appear on every project you start. He is the face of Scratch. If you don't want to use him in your project, it's OK! You can select whichever sprite you would like. But Scratch Cat will always appear with a new project to get you started.

alien head—Click to open the Sprite Library and select a sprite. All sprites are sorted alphabetically. You can choose anything from a dinosaur sprite to cheesy puffs to an airplane.

 paintbrush—Click on the paintbrush to open the paint tools and create your own sprite.

 folder—Click on the folder to upload an image from your computer to use as a sprite.

 camera—Click on the camera to use a picture from your computer as a sprite. A box will pop up asking to access the camera. Press *allow* to let Scratch access your computer's camera.

NAME YOUR SPRITE HERE

Click the blue ⓘ to open the sprite's information.

If a sprite is flipping upside down, change its rotation style here.

When you have selected a sprite, you will see three tabs in the top right corner: **Scripts**, **Costumes**, and **Sounds**.

Code blocks are color coded. To figure out which category a certain block is in, look at the color of the block and match it with the category.

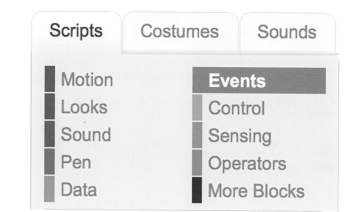

SCRIPTS TAB:

The Scripts tab is where you will create the code for all your projects. When you click on the Scripts tab, you will have access to the different code blocks needed to create projects.

Motion: These blocks are used to create movement. Using these blocks, you can tell your sprite to move around the screen, go to a particular place, turn, and more.

Looks: Here you will find the code needed to make your sprite or project change colors, grow, shrink, swap backgrounds, switch costumes, and much more! You can even code your sprite to say or think certain things. (When you code it with a *say* block, a speech bubble will appear above the sprite. The *say* and *think* blocks are here rather than in **Sound** because your sprite won't actually make any noise with these two blocks.)

Sound: Turn up the volume! The blocks in this category add sound to your sprites and/or background.

Pen: These blocks allow your sprites to draw lines wherever they move. (For example, if your sprite moves, then turns 90 degrees four times, you can create a square.) The size, color, and shade of the pen can also be programmed here.

Data: Here you can create variables to use within a project. A variable is a value that can be changed throughout the course of a project. (For example, you can use a variable for the number of lives a sprite has in a game.)

Events: These are your start commands. All code has a start command. This tells the program when it needs to start. These blocks will be the first piece used in any code you write. The most commonly used start command in this book will be the green flag.

Control: These blocks control how long certain things happen and if one thing causes another to start. There are repeat loops, wait commands, cloning blocks, and *if then* statements called conditional statements. (For example *if* a sprite touches a certain color, *then* it needs to react in a certain way.) The *if then* conditional block will be one of the most used in this book.

Sensing: These blocks are used to detect things—like touching a certain sprite or color—in your code. They are often paired with the *if then* conditional block from Control. (For example, "If touching color blue, then the sprite jumps three times.")

Operators: These code blocks are used to combine codes or set a random range for something within a set of code. They will always be combined with other code blocks when used.

More Blocks: You won't see any blocks in this category at first—that's because you must create any blocks that go here. It can be helpful to create a block when you need to use a big piece of code repeatedly in a set of commands.

In Scratch, code blocks snap together like puzzle pieces. Simply drag the blocks together to make them attach. The code you create will run in whatever order you place the blocks. To take the blocks apart, pull from the bottom and down. If you remove a single piece, all the blocks attached below will stay connected to that piece. (You must pull each one off from the bottom.) To throw away a block you no longer want or need, drag it back to the category you originally selected it from and let go.

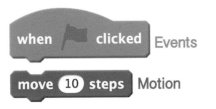

The code block on the right starts with the green flag being clicked. (This is the start command.) Next the sprite will say "Hello!" for two seconds. Once the two seconds have passed, the sprite will move 10 steps.

COSTUMES:

Here you can edit a sprite's appearance. You can also create your own sprite, or add a new costume to an existing sprite. Different costumes can be used to make it look like a sprite is moving. (Some sprites—like Scratch Cat—automatically come with more than one costume.) Multiple costumes are key to making your sprite look animated. Keep in mind that while you may have multiple costumes, there is still only one sprite!

You can name your costumes here.

When you open the Costumes tab, you will see tools you can use to customize your sprite.

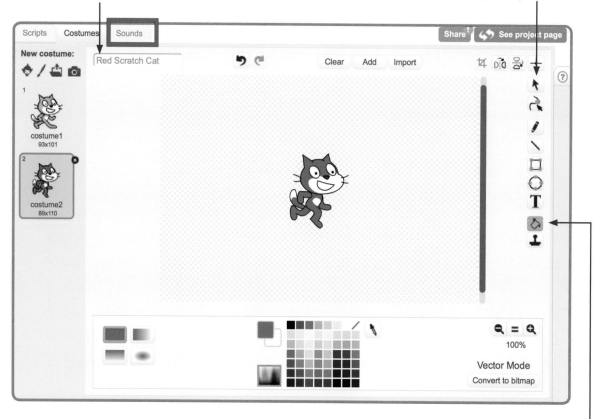

For this costume we used the paint bucket to make Scratch Cat red instead of his usual orange.

SOUNDS:

Once you've started a project, you can add sounds to your creation. To add a sound to a project, first select the sound from the library. You will later add it into the project through coding.

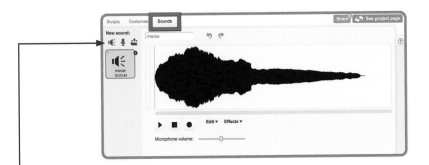

Each sprite comes with its own sound. Scratch Cat's sound is *meow*. Other sprites usually come with simple sounds like *pop*. Sprites that are imported or created using the graphic design tools do not have any sounds attached. To add a sound from the library, click on the speaker button.

SOUND LIBRARY:

Sound Library

Category
All
Animal
Effects
Electronic
Human
Instruments
Music Loops
Musical Notes
Percussion
Vocals

afro string alien creak1 alien creak2 bass beatbox beat box1 beat box2

bell cymbal bell toll bird birthday bells birthday boing

bubbles buzz whir car passing cave chee chee cheer

chomp chord clap beatbox clapping computer beeps1 computer beeps2

OK   Cancel

You can search for sounds easily by using the categories on the left side. The sounds within the library are sorted alphabetically to make them easier to find.

BACKDROPS:

Just like with sprites, there are lots of ways to access backdrops in Scratch and make them your own. You can select, create, upload, or snap a picture. The buttons used to create a new backdrop can be found on the bottom left corner of your screen, under the sprites section. There are four buttons you will use:

 mountain landscape—This icon opens the Backdrop Library so you can select a backdrop.

 paintbrush—This icon opens the paint tools, allowing you to create and name your own background.

 folder—This icon lets you upload an image from your computer to use as a background.

 camera—This icon lets you take a picture from your computer and use it as a background. (Note: When you click the camera, a pop-up box will ask to access the camera. Press *allow* to use the camera to create a backdrop.)

Backdrops are sorted by category and alphabetically in the Backdrop Library.

BACKDROP LIBRARY:

How to Use the Drawing Tools

One of the best parts about coding with Scratch is your ability to create your own backdrops and sprites. There are endless possibilities! If you're having trouble finding the perfect sprite or background for your project, stop hunting for it and just make it!

BITMAP MODE VS. VECTOR MODE

There are two different modes you can use for creating your own backgrounds and sprites—**bitmap** or **vector**.

Convert to bitmap

Bitmap mode makes it easy to fill in simple backgrounds and shapes. If you need to create a quick shape or background, use the design tools in this mode. (But keep in mind that if you make a shape and need to resize it later, bitmap mode won't allow it.)

Convert to vector

Vector mode has many of the same tools but is more flexible. It lets you reshape or resize shapes you've made. You can also create another shape and then go back to a previous one to move it. Vector is more useful for detailed backgrounds and sprites.

Bitmap design tools appear on the left of the backdrop screen.

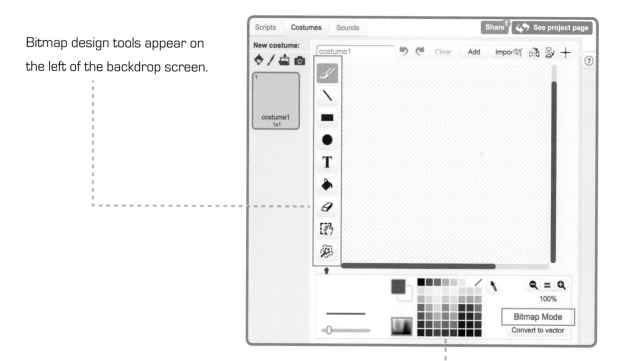

Colors will always show on the bottom of your creation screen.

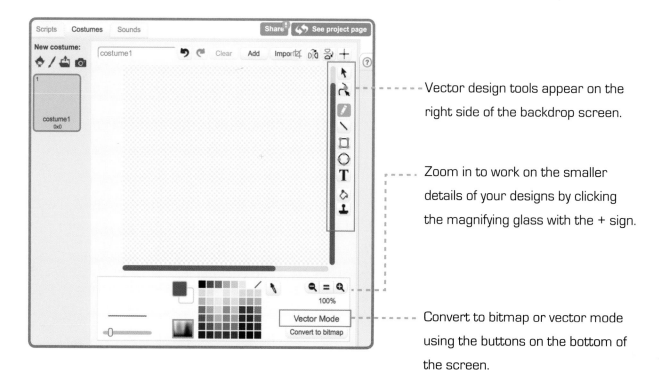

Vector design tools appear on the right side of the backdrop screen.

Zoom in to work on the smaller details of your designs by clicking the magnifying glass with the + sign.

Convert to bitmap or vector mode using the buttons on the bottom of the screen.

For details on what each tool does, keep reading!

BITMAP MODE TOOLS:

paintbrush—Use the paintbrush tool to draw freehand. Click and drag the mouse around to paint. Change the thickness of the paintbrush using the width slider on the bottom left of the screen.

line—Use this tool to draw lines. Click and drag the mouse until the line is your desired length. To create a perfectly straight line, press and hold shift while drawing.

rectangle—Click the rectangle icon, then drag the mouse diagonally to create a rectangle. (Once you've selected this tool, you can choose either a hollow or filled-in rectangle at the bottom of the screen.) To make a perfect square, hold down shift while creating the shape.

circle—Click the circle icon, then drag the mouse diagonally to create a circle. (Once you've selected this tool, you can select either a hollow or filled-in circle at the bottom of the screen.) To make a perfect circle, hold down shift while creating the shape.

text—Select the T icon to add text to your design. Click inside the box until you see a cursor, then select the color and font you'd like at the bottom of the screen. To make the text larger, click out of the text box, then stretch the text using the sizing dots.

paint bucket—Use this tool to fill in the background or a shape with a certain color. If you're filling in a shape, be sure that there are no gaps in the drawing, otherwise the paint will leak out and fill the entire page! (You may need to zoom in to see if there are any gaps—sometimes they're hard to spot!)

eraser—Use this tool to remove things from your project. Just click and drag the mouse across the object you want to remove. To change the size of the eraser, use the scroll bar on the bottom of the screen.

 grabber—Use the grabber to delete, move, or stretch something. Just drag a box around the item and get to work!

 magic wand—Use the magic wand to remove backgrounds on any images you've uploaded.

 stamp—Use the stamp to duplicate something you've made.

Line width:

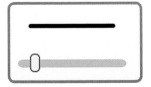

Filled-in or hollow shape:

Eraser size:

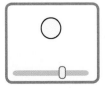

VECTOR MODE:

mouse pointer—Use the pointer to reselect a shape after you've created it. Once you select the shape, you can resize, move, or delete it.

reshape—The reshape tool lets you make changes to a circle or square you've already created. For details on how to use this tool, check out the next page!

pencil—Use this tool to draw freehand. Change the thickness of the line using the scrollbar at the bottom of the screen.

line—Use this tool to draw lines in your project. Click and drag the mouse until the line is your desired length. To create a perfectly straight line, press and hold shift while creating drawing.

square—Click the square icon, then drag the mouse diagonally to create a square. (Once you've selected this tool, you can choose either a hollow or filled-in square at the bottom of the screen.) To make a perfect square, press and hold down shift while creating the shape.

circle—Click the circle icon, then drag the mouse diagonally to create a circle. (Once you've selected this tool, you can choose either a hollow or filled-in circle at the bottom of the screen.) To make a perfect circle, press and hold shift while creating the shape.

text—Select the T icon to add a text box to your design. Click inside the box until you see a cursor, then select the color and font you'd like at the bottom of the screen. To make the text larger, click out of the text box, then stretch the text using the sizing dots.

paint bucket—Use the paint bucket to color in shapes you've created. (Keep in mind the paint bucket won't fill in the entire background unless you make a big square to fill it. It won't fill in images you've drawn unless it is a closed shape.)

stamp—Use the stamp to duplicate different shapes. This is helpful when you want two shapes to be identical, like a pair of eyes!

up arrow/down arrow—These tools move objects forward or behind other shapes in a drawing. They will appear when you have more than one image in the creation space. The up arrow brings an object forward a layer, and the down arrow moves something back a layer. (For example, if you made a large shape and want it behind a smaller shape, click the down arrow to send it back a layer so the smaller shape is on top.)

group—Use this tool when you have used multiple shapes to create something and you'd like them all to move as one object. Use the mouse pointer to draw a box around the shapes, then click this icon to group them together.

ungroup—Use this tool to separate objects or shapes that are grouped together.

USING THE RESHAPE TOOL

To use the reshape tool, be sure that you made your circle or square in vector mode. (If you created it in bitmap, you won't be able to reshape it.)

 Create a shape.

 Click the reshape icon, and then click on the shape you made. Reshape dots will appear.

 Push or pull the reshape dots until you have your desired shape.

MAKING AN EYEBALL:

An eye may seem like a basic shape, but creating one involves a few different tools. To make an eyeball, click on the paintbrush in the sprite toolbar to draw your own sprite.

paintbrush

Click *Convert to vector* at the bottom right of the screen.

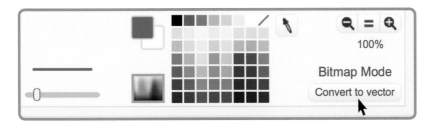

Use the circle tool to draw and layer three circles: one large white circle, one medium black circle, and one small white circle. Make sure all three are filled in, and layer them like this:

 Check that you are using vector mode so you can move the circles around as needed!

 When you finish drawing the eye, click on the mouse pointer and draw a box around it.

Click the group icon so you can move, shrink, or grow all three circles as one eye.

Let's use some more shapes to create this cute little guy!

Create a red circle and place the eye on top of it.

Draw a small smile using the black pencil. (You can increase the thickness of the line using the sliding toolbar at the bottom left.)

Draw a big red oval for the body. Then using the circle tool, create a thin oval for the right arm. Use the top circle to rotate the oval slightly, then drag it into position on the body.

Using the duplicate tool, make an identical arm for the other side. Click the *flip left-right* icon at the top right to rotate the arm in the correct direction. Drag it to the opposite side of the body.

TIP:

Don't be afraid to use the undo and redo arrows if you make a mistake! They can be very helpful. As you work through the projects to come, you'll be creating lots of sprites and backdrops. Refer to this page for help if you ever get lost.

THE GOAL:

Make a pen that can be moved around the screen to create a drawing. Pick from either a pencil or fun rainbow pen!

LET'S GET STARTED!

STEP 1: Start a new project and delete Scratch Cat. Then select three button sprites from the Sprite Library. (You can also choose one button sprite and use the stamp tool to duplicate it twice.) Drag the sprites so they are stacked along the right side of your background. (You will be drawing all over the background, so you don't want them to get in the way of your art!)

scissors   Sprite Library   Button3   Button2   Button4

STEP 2: Open the Sprite Library again and select the sprite you'd like to use as the drawing tool in your project. (For this project, we're using the pencil sprite.)

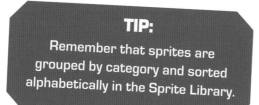

TIP:
Remember that sprites are grouped by category and sorted alphabetically in the Sprite Library.

STEP 3: Open the Costumes tab on each of the button sprites to customize it. Use the paint bucket to fill in each button using a different color. Use the text tool to create a text box inside each button.

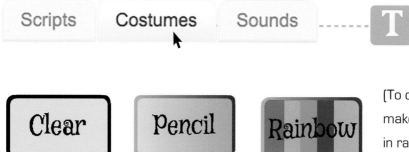

(To create the rainbow effect, make multiple filled-in rectangles in rainbow colors and put them inside the button. Then add the text on top!)

STEP 4: Open each sprite's information tab by clicking the small blue *i* and name the buttons *clear*, *rainbow*, and *pencil*. Name your drawing tool (in this case, the pencil) *magic pen*.

TIP:

If the paint bucket isn't successfully filling in the whole background, make sure you're in bitmap mode at the bottom right of your screen.

STEP 5: Click on the paintbrush icon to create a new backdrop. Use the paint bucket to fill in the background with a solid color and use the text tool to type the words *magic pen*. (Keep it simple—the background is designed to be drawn on when the project is completed.)

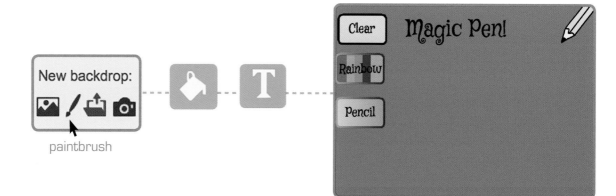

paintbrush

STEP 6: Add this code to the backdrop under the Scripts tab.

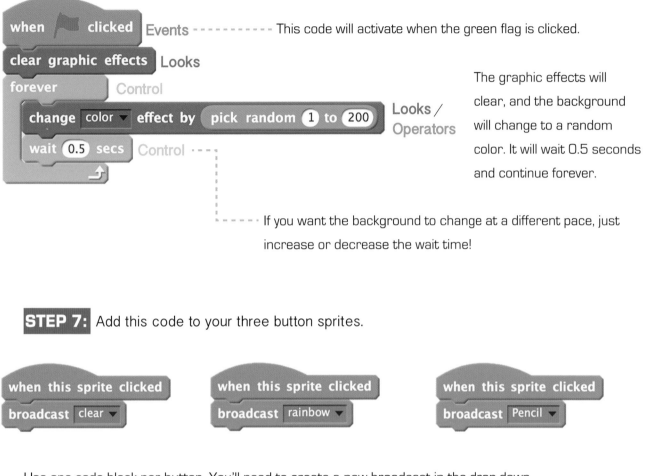

when [flag] clicked — Events · · · · · · · · · This code will activate when the green flag is clicked.

clear graphic effects — Looks

forever — Control

change color effect by (pick random 1 to 200) — Looks / Operators

wait 0.5 secs — Control

The graphic effects will clear, and the background will change to a random color. It will wait 0.5 seconds and continue forever.

· · · · · · If you want the background to change at a different pace, just increase or decrease the wait time!

STEP 7: Add this code to your three button sprites.

when this sprite clicked
broadcast clear ▼

when this sprite clicked
broadcast rainbow ▼

when this sprite clicked
broadcast Pencil ▼

Use one code block per button. You'll need to create a new broadcast in the drop-down menu for each. (A broadcast is like sending a message. You'll create the broadcast to be sent, and later you'll code other sprites to activate a certain code when the broadcast has been received.) Name the broadcast to match your button.

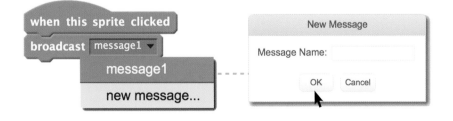

when this sprite clicked
broadcast message1 ▼
  message1
  new message...

New Message

Message Name:

OK   Cancel

Use the broadcast block in Events and create a new message to make these blocks.

Add the following code blocks to the Scripts tab of your magic pen sprite.

When the *clear* message is received from the clear button, all graphic effects (drawing) will clear.

When the space bar is pressed, all code will stop. The pen won't follow the mouse pointer anymore.

When the pencil broadcast is received, the pen will change its size to a small pencil-like size and set its color to purple. Then it will forever follow the mouse and have the pen down so it can draw.

When the rainbow broadcast is received, the pen will change its size to 1 so it starts tiny. Then it will go to the mouse pointer. The pen will go down and the pen color and size will continue to forever change, causing the rainbow color to show and pen size to gradually increase*.

*If you don't want the pen to grow larger and would prefer just the rainbow ink, just take out the *change pen size by* block.

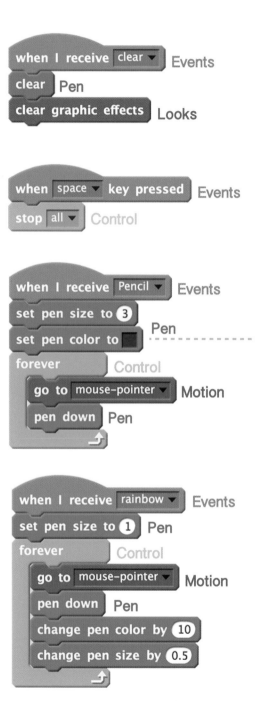

WHAT IS THE PEN CATEGORY IN SCRIPTS?

The *pen down* code block lets sprites draw lines wherever they move. Think about it as though every sprite has a pen hidden inside. You can code the pen to appear and tell it when to disappear into the sprite again so it will stop making a line when it moves. You can also code the color and size of the pen. Cool, right?

TIP:

Remember, to select the color for the *set pen color to* block, click inside the square. A small white finger cursor will appear. When the cursor appears, move it over to the color you'd like to select and click on it.

See project page

You're all set! View your project in full-screen mode to start drawing. Select the color of your choice, then move your mouse to create your own work of art! Click the space bar to stop drawing and the clear button to erase. See the finished project here: https://scratch.mit.edu/projects/125092281/

Bouncing Gummy Bears

THE PROJECT:

Create a gummy bear that will bounce when you click on it. You'll make several different costumes and code the bear to switch through them to make it look like it's moving.

LET'S GET STARTED!

STEP 1: Open a new project screen and delete Scratch Cat. You won't need him here. Then use paintbrush in the drawing tools to draw a big gummy bear sprite. Make sure to use the drawing tools in **vector mode** since you'll need to adjust the gummy bear's size.

scissors   paintbrush   Convert to vector

Create the gummy bear's head using the filled-in circle tool. Use the same tool to draw the ears, reshaping them slightly. (Save time by duplicating the first ear to make the second. Use the *flip left-right* icon, like you did on page 20, to flip the ear.) Continue using the circle tool to draw the body, which will be more of an oval. Draw the paws, this time using the outlined circle. Choose a slightly darker red for the outline so the paws are visible. Then use the paint bucket tool to fill in the paws so they match the body and ears.

Duplicate the paw using the stamp tool until you have four paws. Arrange them on the bear's body.

Using the same darker red, select the pencil tool and add the mouth, nose, and ear details. Then use the circle tool to draw a white circle for the eyes. (You'll need to reshape it slightly to match what you see here.) Add a large black circle and smaller white circle to the center of the eye.

TIP:
It will help to group all the pieces of the eye together and duplicate it so the second eye is identical to the first!

STEP 2: To make it look like the gummy bear is being squished, you'll need to create multiple costumes for your sprite. Each costume will have a very slight change. To start, duplicate the gummy bear's first costume so you have an exact copy. (This new costume will automatically be named *costume2*.)

costume1
168x300

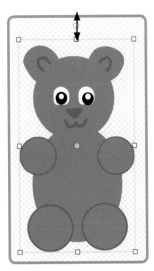

Working in *costume2*, use the pointer tool to draw a box around the entire bear and shrink him just a little. Then click on just the head and reshape it to look slightly squished. The difference should be so small it is hardly noticeable! Duplicate *costume2* to create *costume3*.

Working in *costume3*, drag a box around the whole bear and shrink him again. Then drag a box around just the eyes. Shrink them a bit using the sizing dots that appear. (Make sure you start

TIP:

If you accidentally select other parts of the bear's body, don't worry! Just click on the drawing screen so the box disappears and try again until you have successfully grabbed just the eyes!

your box in the drawing area—outside the bear's body—so you don't move anything else.) Each time you duplicate the costume, the part you squish down will be farther down the bear's body, just like if you squished it with your finger. Duplicate *costume3* to make *costume4*.

Working in *costume4*, drag a box around the whole bear again and shrink him. Then shrink just his top paws!

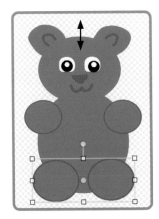

Duplicate *costume4* to create *costume5*.

Working in *costume5*, draw a box around the entire bear and shrink him slightly. Then do the same to just the bottom paws.

STEP 3: You should now have five costumes total. So far the costumes have squished the bear down little by little. Now it's time to start building him back up. You don't need to make any further changes to the bear. You will now duplicate the costumes in reverse order.

Duplicate *costume4* again to create *costume6*. (Use *costume4* because it is just slightly taller than *costume5*.)

Duplicate *costume3* to create *costume7*.

Finally, duplicate *costume2* to make *costume8*.

STEP 4: Create a new backdrop and use the paint bucket to fill it in with any color and effect you like.

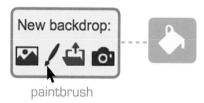

paintbrush

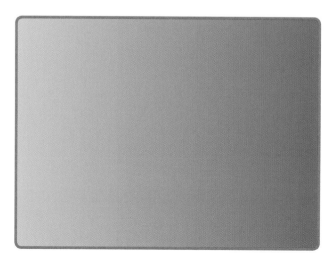

New costume:

1 costume1
168x300

2 costume2
168x297

3 costume3
168x279

4 costume4
168x265

5 costume5
168x253

6 costume6
174x272

7 costume7
174x286

8 costume8
174x305

9

STEP 5: Add this code to the gummy bear sprite's Scripts tab. Then open the sprite's information and name it *red gummy bear*.

```
when this sprite clicked          Events
switch costume to costume1        Looks  - - - -
play sound boing                  Sound
repeat 8                          Control
    next costume                  Looks
```

This code will activate when the gummy bear sprite is clicked. The costume will start on *costume1*, then it will play the sound *boing* and repeat through the costumes eight times, ending at the eighth costume.

You'll need to go into the Sound Library and add the *boing* sound effect before you can select it in the drop-down menu of the **Sound** block.

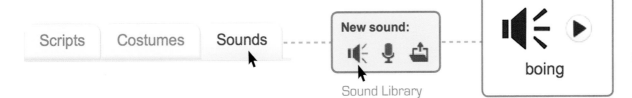

| Scripts | Costumes | Sounds |

New sound:

Sound Library

boing

New costume:

costume1
168x300

costume2
168x297

costume3
168x279

costume4
168x265

costume5
168x253

costume6
168x265

costume7
168x279

costume8
168x297

STEP 6: To make your project more complex, add another bear. Use the stamp tool to duplicate the *red gummy bear* sprite; name the new sprite *green gummy bear*. Then open the Costumes tab and use the paint bucket to fill in the new gummy bear so it's all green. Use a darker green for any details, like the mouth and ears.

shrink tool

Use the shrink tool to shrink down *green gummy bear* sprite if you want it to be smaller. Now you'll have two bouncing gummy bears! All lined up, your costumes should look like this—there will be eight total:

You're finished! Click on the *see project page* button at the top right to view your finished project. Click on your gummy bear to watch him shrink and grow! See the finished project here: https://scratch.mit.edu/projects/174282643/

THE PROJECT:

Create a parrot that will soar through the air by flapping its wings!

LET'S GET STARTED!

STEP 1: Open a new project and name it. Delete Scratch Cat, then use the paintbrush to create a new sprite. (Be sure to switch to **vector mode** before drawing the parrot. You'll need to be able to change it later.)

scissors   paintbrush

Use the circle tool to draw the parrot's body. Select the filled-in circle option at the bottom left of the screen and choose the body color. (We used red.) Make the body more of an oval shape. Then use the same tool to create the parrot's wings. You'll need to draw multiple oval shapes—one big oval for the wing and lots of small ovals for the feathers. We've used the colors red, white, and blue. (Use the stamp tool in your vector toolbar to duplicate the smaller circles for the feathers and rotate them as needed.)

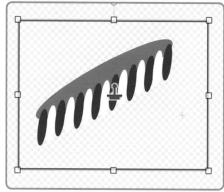

When you have one wing created, draw a box around it and use the grouping tool to group all the pieces together. Then you can easily duplicate the wing. Flip it using the *flip image* tool at the top. You should now have two identical wings.

Drag the wings onto opposite sides of the parrot's body.

 To create the parrot's face, use the circle tool to draw an oval. Make it the same color as the parrot's body. Then use a different color to draw a smaller circle. Place it on top of the larger circle.

To make the eye, draw a white circle outlined in black. Reshape it slightly to match what you see here, then add the black circle and smaller white circle to the inside. Draw a box around the eye and then group all the pieces together before dragging it into position.

Use the circle tool to draw an oval for the beak, then reshape it to be more beak like. Finally, use the pencil tool to draw the parrot's claws. (Your beak and claws should be the same color.)

STEP 2: To make it look like the parrot is flying through the sky, you'll need to create multiple costumes. The wings will be in a slightly different position in each costume. (If you didn't group the pieces of the wings together when you made the sprite, do that now.) Start off by duplicating the first parrot costume using the stamp tool. This will create *costume2*.

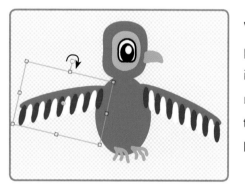

Working in *costume2*, use the mouse pointer tool and click on the wing to select it. Then use the small dot on the top to rotate the wing up slightly. Do the same thing on the other wing. The difference will hardly be noticeable at first!

Continue duplicating the parrot costume until you have 10 costumes. Working through each costume (in order) rotate the wings slightly more than in the previous costume. By *costume10*, the wings will be pointing up.

STEP 3: Use the paintbrush in the backdrop tools to create a new backdrop. Then use the tools in your toolbar to draw a backdrop that looks like the sky. (It's OK to draw your backdrop in bitmap mode since you won't be changing it.) Don't forget to add clouds and a sun!

STEP 4: Add the below code blocks to your parrot sprite. This code will tell the parrot to move using the arrow keys and switch through its costumes to make it look like the wings are flapping.

The X and Y in the **Motion** block refers to the X and Y axes of a coordinate plane. The X axis runs horizontally (left and right). The Y axis runs vertically (up and down). If you have a positive Y coordinate it will be in the upper half of the plane. A negative Y coordinate will be found on the lower half. A positive X coordinate will be found on the right side. A negative X coordinate will be found on the left side.

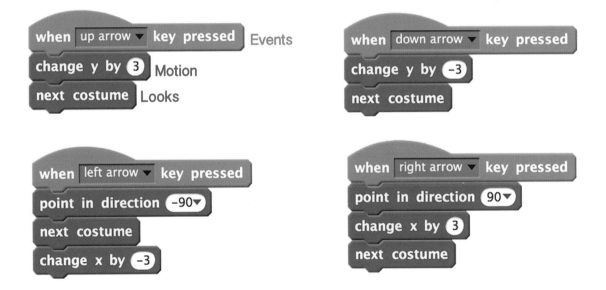

You're finished! View your project in full-screen mode, and use the arrow keys to watch your parrot fly around the page. See the finished project here: https://scratch.mit.edu/projects/174286343/

ALL About You Presentation

THE PROJECT:

Click the different buttons to share information about yourself in a fun new way!

LET'S GET STARTED!

STEP 1: Open a new project and create a new backdrop. (Go ahead and delete Scratch Cat—we won't need him for this presentation.) This will be your start screen. Use the paint bucket and text box tools to edit the background, filling it in with a solid color and adding text to the background. Name it *All About Me*.

scissors   paintbrush

Think about what types of things you want to share about yourself. We've used favorite color, animal, candy, food, sport, and season. If you want to pick more favorites or replace an example with something else, go for it! The awesome part about coding is that you can personalize everything. This project is all about YOU, so change the categories to fit your personality.

STEP 2: Add six button sprites from the Sprite Library. (You can also add one button sprite and use the stamp tool to duplicate it five times.) Once you have your button sprites, open the Costumes tab for each and customize it with a category. (We've used candy, season, food, color, sport, and animal.)

Sprite Library

Use the paint bucket and text tool to customize the button sprites. (Click the ⓘ to open the sprite's information box and name each one.)

You can arrange your buttons on your start screen however you'd like!

STEP 3: Use the paintbrush icon in your backdrop toolbar to make unique backdrops for each of your six buttons. Add your own answer for each category you created. You will create new backdrops, one per button, until you have a total of seven, including your *All About Me* screen! Be sure to name each background to match the button it goes with. (Example: The pizza background should be labeled *food* to match your *food* button.)

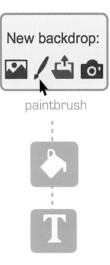

New backdrop:

paintbrush

STEP 4: Add the below code block to all your button sprites. (Look at page 7 for a quick tip on how to copy code from one sprite to another.)

This code is activated when the button sprite is clicked. When the button is clicked, the *pop* sound will play and the background will switch. Then a hide broadcast will be sent to all the button sprites, three seconds will pass, and the background will switch back to the *All About Me* backdrop.

Don't forget to update the backdrop name in the *switch backdrop to* **Looks** block so it matches the button sprite you're coding. (For example, the above code block belongs on the candy button sprite.) You'll also need to create a new broadcast using the drop-down menu in the **Events** block. This broadcast won't change from sprite to sprite. Once it has been created, it will stay the same on all.

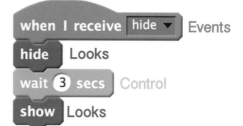

When the hide broadcast is received, the button sprites hide, wait for 3 seconds, and show back up.

To add even more to this project, spice up the backgrounds by drawing different pictures on them, like the cotton candy and pizza in step 3. You could even add special sounds for each button and code them to play when the backgrounds switch. Play around with it and have fun creating a project that's all about YOU! See the finished project here: https://scratch.mit.edu/projects/174293179/

THE PROJECT:

Click the space bar to move through this how-to project on making yummy spaghetti. Click on the images below each step to see them move.

LET'S GET STARTED!

STEP 1: Start a new project, delete Scratch Cat, and use the paintbrush icon to create your own intro screen. On this backdrop, describe what your tutorial will be. (Ours is *How to Make Spaghetti*.) At the bottom of the screen, add a note that says *click the space bar to begin*. When you're finished, name this backdrop *Start Screen*.

scissors

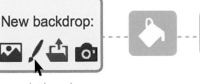

paintbrush

Use the paint bucket and text tools to edit your background, adding the color and text.

Feel free to draw some extra pictures to this backdrop; it can be as simple or crazy as you'd like!

To create this two-color effect, select two colors when filling in the paint bucket. Then select the fill type you'd like in the bottom left corner. Use the drop-down menu on the bottom left to change the font if you'd like.

How to Make Spaghetti

CLICK THE SPACE BAR TO BEGIN.

STEP 2: Add this code to the Scripts tab of your backdrop. When the green flag is clicked, the backdrop will switch to your start screen. When space bar is pressed, it will go to next backdrop.

when 🏴 clicked Events

switch backdrop to start screen ▼ Looks

when space ▼ key pressed

next backdrop

STEP 3: Use the paintbrush in the backdrop toolbar to make new backdrops for the steps of your tutorial. Keep it to just two steps per page—you'll need to leave room for the animated sprites you'll add later. Create your backdrop(s) in vector mode so you can change the text from backdrop to backdrop.

New backdrop: 🖼 ✏ ⬆ 📷 - - - - Convert to vector

Backdrop Library

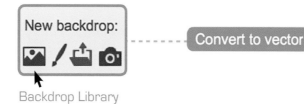

Steps:
1. Boil water in a pot.

2. Place spaghetti in boiling water.

Name the first screen *Steps*. Then use the stamp tool at the top of the screen to duplicate this backdrop. Change the steps/instructions on the background. This backdrop will automatically be named *Steps2*. Duplicate and change the steps again for *Steps3**.

*If your tutorial requires more steps than this example, keep going! You can have as many pages as you need. Just be sure to name each step so you can keep them straight later.

STEP 4: Use the paintbrush icon to create the sprites for your steps. The first step in making spaghetti is to boil a pot of water. You'll need a pot sprite! Use vector mode so you can easily make changes to the sprite later.

paintbrush

Start with a simple pot. Use the circle tool to draw a circle outlined in gray and filled in with blue (for the water). Then draw a curved square for the bottom and a rectangle for the handle. (You may need to rotate the rectangle slightly, or use the *forward a layer/back a layer* tools to layer things correctly.) Name the finished sprite *pot*.

STEP 5: Duplicate the pot costume and add flames. Name this costume *flame 1*.

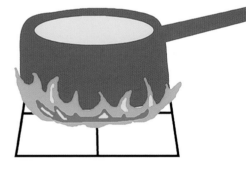

Duplicate the *flame 1* costume and change the flames a bit. Add small gray dots that look like bubbles to the water. (These represent the water boiling.) This costume will automatically be named *flame 2*.

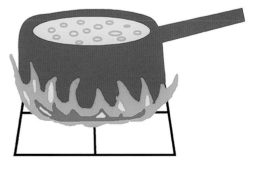

Duplicate *flame 2*; move the bubbles around a bit and adjust the flame slightly to create *flame 3*. Repeat this process once more to create *flame 4*.

STEP 6: Add the code below onto the pot sprite.

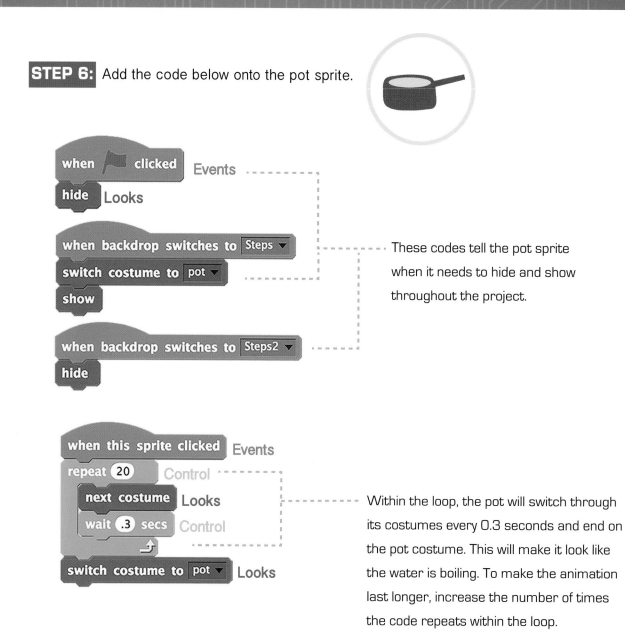

```
when [flag] clicked    Events
hide   Looks
```

```
when backdrop switches to Steps ▼
switch costume to pot ▼
show
```

```
when backdrop switches to Steps2 ▼
hide
```

These codes tell the pot sprite when it needs to hide and show throughout the project.

```
when this sprite clicked   Events
repeat 20        Control
    next costume   Looks
    wait .3 secs   Control
switch costume to pot ▼   Looks
```

Within the loop, the pot will switch through its costumes every 0.3 seconds and end on the pot costume. This will make it look like the water is boiling. To make the animation last longer, increase the number of times the code repeats within the loop.

STEP 7: Use the paintbrush icon in the sprite toolbar to draw a spaghetti sprite. Use the drawing tools to make long, straight lines to look like uncooked spaghetti. When you're finished, open the sprite's information and name it *raw spaghetti*.

paintbrush

STEP 8: Add the code below to the *raw spaghetti* sprite.

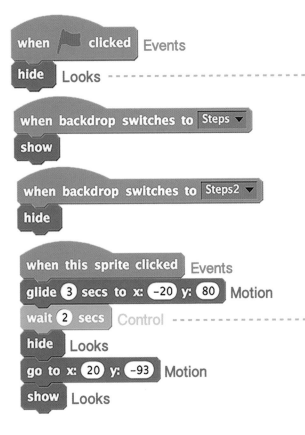

These blocks tell the *raw spaghetti* sprite to hide when the green flag is clicked and then to show or hide when the backdrop switches to different steps.

This code will activate when the sprite is clicked. It will then slowly glide up to where the pot sprite is. (To figure out the exact coordinates, drag the *raw spaghetti* sprite to the *pot* sprite on the screen. The code block coordinates will automatically update.) The *raw spaghetti* sprite will then wait two seconds, hide, and go back to its original spot. (For the X and Y coordinates here, drag the spaghetti back and the *go to* block will update.)

STEP 9: Arrange your sprites on the *Steps* backdrop to match the image below.

STEP 10: Use the paintbrush icon in the sprite toolbar to draw a clock sprite. Use the drawing tools in vector mode.

paintbrush

Use the circle tool to create a circle outlined in black and filled in white. Then add a circle to the middle and draw two lines coming out for the minute and hour hands. Use the pencil tool to make the notches for the hours.

When you finish the first costume, duplicate it and change the minute hand slightly. Keep duplicating and rotating the minute hand until you have a total of four costumes. (They will automatically name themselves *costume1*, *costume2*, *costume3*, and *costume4*.)

STEP 11: Click on the paintbrush icon and use the vector drawing tools to create a new sprite that looks like plain cooked spaghetti on a plate.

paintbrush

Convert to vector

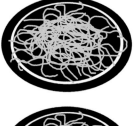

To make the plate for the pasta, use a filled-in circle. Then add squiggles for the pasta.

Duplicate the first costume and add marinara sauce for the second costume. (Draw a closed-off shape and fill it in for the sauce.)

Duplicate the second costume and add cheese for the final cooked spaghetti costume. (Add dots for the cheese using the pencil tool.)

Name the costumes *plated pasta*, *pasta sauce*, and *finished*.

STEP 12: Place the clock and cooked spaghetti on the appropriate backdrops. (To do this, select the backdrop in the backdrop section, then drag the sprite to the correct spot on your creation screen.

Don't worry if there are other sprites on the screen when you do this. You'll code them to disappear on screens you don't want them on later.)

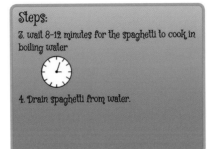

Steps:
3. wait 8-12 minutes for the spaghetti to cook in boiling water

4. Drain spaghetti from water.

Steps:
5. Place spaghetti on a plate with marinara sauce and cheese.

ENJOY!

STEP 13: Add this code to the *cooked spaghetti* sprite.

These blocks tell the sprite when to hide and show, depending on the step. The longer code with the repeat block animates the sprite by switching through its costumes.

If you'd like the pasta to switch through the costumes faster, change the wait time to a smaller number!

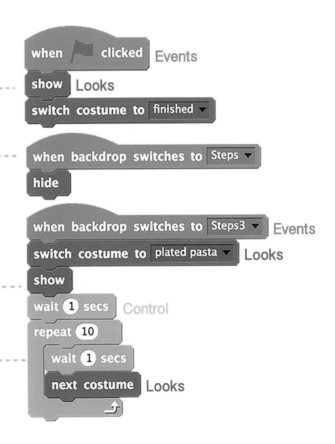

STEP 14: Add the below code to the *clock* sprite.

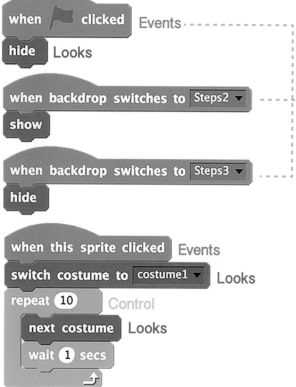

These blocks tell the clock sprite when to hide and show, depending on the step.

The longer code with the repeat Control block animates the clock by switching through its costumes.

TIP:
If you're ever confused by a direction or need extra help, click on the finished project link at the end of the project. You can open the project online and see all the code for clarification!

You're ready to teach people how to make spaghetti! View your finished project and use the space bar to move through the steps. See the finished project here: https://scratch.mit.edu/projects/174294795/

Read More

Wainewright, Max. *Code Your Own Games!: 20 Games to Create with Scratch*. New York, NY. Sterling Children's Books, 2017.

Ziter, Rachel. *Coding in Scratch for Beginners: 4D An Augmented Reading Experience*. North Mankato, Minn.: Capstone Press, 2018.

Ziter, Rachel. *Making Music from Scratch: 4D An Augmented Reading Experience*. North Mankato, Minn.: Capstone Press, 2019.

Makerspace Tips

Download tips and tricks for using this book and others in a library makerspace.

Visit www.capstonepub.com/dabblelabresources

Internet Sites

Use Facthound to find Internet sites related to this book.

Visit www.facthound.com

Just type in 9781515766599 and go.

Coding Glossary

bitmap mode: The drawing tools in this mode make it easy to fill in backgrounds and shapes. If you are making a quick shape or basic background, bitmap mode is a good choice. (Keep in mind that if you need to go back and resize a shape later, bitmap mode won't allow it.) To change between bitmap and vector mode, use the buttons on the bottom right of the design screen.

broadcast: These code blocks can be found in the Events category of the Scripts tab. A broadcast is like sending a message.

coding: Coding is the language used to communicate with a computer. By creating a set of code, you are writing directions in a language that the computer can follow. Code is very specific! Without code, computers wouldn't know how to do anything.

conditional statement: A conditional statement is used in code when you need one thing to happen, but only if another does. (For example: If _____ happens, then _____ needs to happen.) These are also called *if then* statements.

Coordinate: A coordinate is an object's exact X-position and Y-position on a coordinate plane. Think of it as a very specific spot!

coordinate plane: A coordinate plane is made up of an X and Y axis. These two axes run perpendicular to each other—one runs up and down, and the other runs right to left. When they meet, the axes create four quadrants.

loop: Loops are used in coding when something needs to happen more than once. Loops can be used with one piece of code or many. The code inside the loop will run (on repeat) in the order it's placed in.

origin: The origin is the middle point of a coordinate plane. This is where the X-coordinate and Y-coordinate both equal zero and the two axes cross.

sequence: Sequence is when something is completed in a specific order. In coding, all programs run in a sequence from top to bottom, meaning the top piece of code will be run first, then the block under it, until the sequence is complete.

sprite: A sprite is any movable character or object used in a Scratch project. Sprites can be selected through the Scratch Library, created using drawing tools, or uploaded from the computer.

variable: A variable is a placeholder for a value and can be made in the Data category of the Scripts tab. The value of a variable can be changed throughout the course of a project. For example, if a variable was used for the number of lives in a game, you could set it to three at the start of a game. Then each time one sprite touches a certain sprite, the lives variable can be coded to decrease by one.

vector mode: The drawing tools in this mode are similar to tools in bitmap mode. However, in vector mode you can create another shape and still go back to a previous one and move it. In this mode, you can also reshape objects that you have made.

X-axis: The X-axis is the axis that runs horizontally (side to side) in a coordinate plane.

Y-axis: The Y-axis is the axis that runs vertically (up and down) in a coordinate plane.

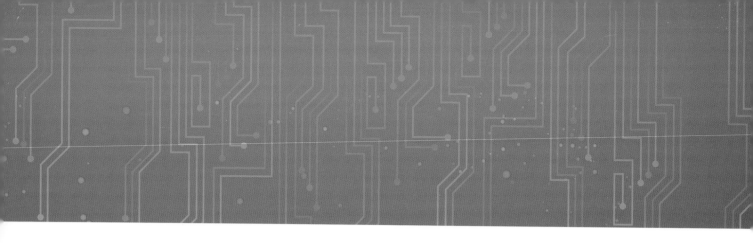

ABOUT THE AUTHOR

Rachel Ziter was raised in Las Vegas, Nevada. She earned a Bachelor of Science in Education and her teaching credentials from Florida Southern College. She has also completed graduate coursework in computer science education at St. Scholastica, as well as professional development in fablab project-based learning at NuVu. Rachel currently works at the Adelson Educational Campus in Las Vegas and is a member of the Tech Team, where she teaches STEM curriculum and instruction, mentors students, and teaches coding and engineering.